SELLING ART ONLINE

THE CREATIVE GUIDE TO TURNING YOUR ARTISTIC WORK INTO CASH

BY
DAVE CONREY

"Art is frightening.

Art isn't pretty. Art isn't painting. Art isn't something you hang on the wall.

Art is what we do when we're truly alive."

– Seth Godin

To book Dave Conrey for speaking engagements, visit www.freshrag.com

For information regarding this book, please visit www.tigerheromedia.com

Second Edition

Designed and Written by Dave Conrey

ISBN 978-0-9904421-0-3

To Leslie, for giving me the power to do what I do.

To Aidan, for giving me the reason.

CONTENTS

INTRODUCTION

WHO SHOULD READ THIS BOOK

WE ARE <u>ALL</u> ARTISTS!

It's true, the title of the book says "art", but this book is not meant strictly for traditional artists. Whether you use paint as your medium, software, watercolor abstracts, digital illustration, or graphic design, this book might be for you. The information contained in these pages is not constrained by mediums or substrates.

If you desire to find ways to spread your work across multiple online platforms in order to reach a wider clientele, then you're in the right place. If you know you want to be online, but not sure which sites offer the best option for displaying your work, this book can help.

If you tell people you're an artist and then shrink when they ask how you make money, this book will give you the ammunition to fight back the naïveté. If people ask, "When are you going to get a *real* job?" now you can tell them you have a job, and it's selling creative awesomeness online.

The online landscape for artists is vast and intimidating. The first priority of this book is to give you the guide through the expansive world of online art sales. By the time you finish this book, with a bit of Internet know-how, you will be exposed to several sites where you can get started selling your work, in short time, and little to no money out of your pocket.

The second priority, and equally important goal of this book, is to motivate and encourage you to find a plan that works for your art, and give you the tools to execute that plan with precision. I wrote this book as a means to help artists, designers, photographers, and other creative individuals take their work to new levels, making more money than ever before.

This is not a get-rich-quick book. I'm not here to preach the virtues of the handmade millionaire. However, there are plenty of individuals in the creative world making good income from their artistic efforts, and you could be one of them.

There is work to be done, so be prepared for it. This is not a walk in the park, but if you're willing to put the time and energy into making something awesome, then the opportunities are yours to take. At the very least, you're making money doing what you love, and moving toward a lifestyle you desire.

If you're tired of your daily grind and wish to find ways to turn your art into cash-money, the answers are here.

THE INTERNET IS ALIVE

Because of the speed at which life on the Internet happens, it is impossible for me to keep up with every little bit of new information coming out about the sites I mention here. I have made notes about changes that have happened from one version of the book to another, but no matter how many adjustments I make, some bit of information will be stagnant by the time this book hits shelves. It's the nature of the digital world, I suppose.

What this means to you is things change. You will find circumstances where something you read here ends up being in conflict with new rules and procedures of the sites in question. Don't be stymied by these changes, but adapt, learn, and grow with them. Whatever you do, do not get caught up in the politics of these changes. Far too often I have seen sites change their operating procedures, and a group of effected sellers go off on rants about how the site is not playing fair, or only building the business on the backs of the creators.

The creators who win in these situations are the ones who do not get bogged down with details, but instead learn how to adapt the changes to their business. The ones who spend their time resisting change end up losing because they spend their time battling the system instead of working on putting up new product. Do you want to fight, or do you want to earn? The choice is yours, but I'll bet you are here to make money.

In the last edition of this book I had all the links in the body of book as they were mentioned. Being a designer at heart, it bothered me how those links broke up the flow of the text. At the back of this book, you'll find a complete list of all the sites and links so you can visit at your leisure. I encourage you to check out all your options first before you commit to any, because again, things could change.

As mentioned above, I try to keep on top of changes, but it's difficult to rewrite and repost for every small change that comes around. The best advice I give is to take what you read here as a primer for how the sites operate and then alter your point of view as needed when new changes occur.

If you do run across something that has changed, and you want to give me a heads up, feel free to drop me an e-mail directly: dave@ freshrag.com.

CHAPTER 1

SO YOU THINK YOU CAN SELL ART?

In the olden days (before the explosion of art on the Internet), artists toiled over their work, expressing their creativity, passion, emotions, hopes, fears, time, and energy onto canvas, paper, or stone. They took the child from the womb and thrust it into the light for strangers to poke and prod, determining completely on personal instinct if the work was worthy of being offered for sale.

Back then, gallery owners and art dealers were gods, praising or shunning artists on a whim. The galleries and dealers developed art movements and the artists complied by creating the kind of work their benefactors determined worthy of display. Who could blame them? If a prominent gallery offered to feature the artist's work on the walls for four weeks to find buyers—and potential future commissions—no artist would turn down the opportunity.

What would happen if the art was not deemed worthy or appropriate? The truth is most artists, designers, illustrators, and photographers never had a chance at any kind of success because their art didn't have the appeal the galleries were interested in. Does that mean the art had no value and no potential for sales? Of course not. There are millions of competent artists, but only so many galleries with only so much wall space.

The alternatives were hawking the art in street fairs or art and craft shows, which might earn them some sales, but usually at a lower price point and reaching a limited number of customers. Being a creative maker before the Internet must have been a painful proposition.

HOW AN AUCTIONEER CHANGED EVERYTHING

Years ago, people were wary of shopping online. Few sites were trusted enough to buy from, and payments were usually processed through traditional means, like checks sent out with order forms, or credit cards given over the phone. I recall a friend telling me once that he would never buy anything on the Internet because of the thieves, bandits, and pirates waiting to bushwhack his personal information.

My first online shopping experience was through eBay. Back then, if you won your bid, you mailed your check or money order to the seller and you hoped they eventually shipped whatever it was they were selling. I believe my first purchase was a back issue of *Ray Gun* magazine. There was no ratings system back then, so I had no recourse if the product was in less-than-quoted condition, but I was happy to experience this amazing new tool for buying other people's junk. I bought all kinds of crap on eBay, some of which I resold to someone later, and some I still have today. Once I tried to buy a katana blade before they stopped allowing weapons on eBay. I remember it like it was yesterday; I missed the winning bid by $1. Hoping the guy had more than one available, I decided to look through his open sales, I realized the sword was a fluke, but what he really sold was his artwork. It was spooky stuff, somewhere between Edvard Munch and J.R.R. Tolkien; not really my style, but I remember thinking how cool it was that you could sell art through this auction website. I knew this would to change the way art was purchased, and galleries were doomed to extinction.

Jump ahead to now and there are more art galleries now than there were in 1996, but now even the galleries are selling art online. They survived and adapted, but the rules had changed. They now had competition from hundreds, if not thousands of sites selling art, including many artists selling their art direct to customers without having to pay fat gallery commissions.

The democratization of selling changed the landscape for artists forever. Many galleries still failed, typically because they did not understand the influence of the Internet. Scoffing at the idea of selling art to people via telecom was an absurd notion to the elite dealers, but the Internet thrives, and those galleries are gone. The galleries that survive do so by embracing the technology and using it to burgeon sales and grow their audience.

And now you can too.

THE BURDEN OF TOO MANY CHOICES

Today, the problem for artists isn't how to get noticed by galleries, but which sites are the best for selling their particular type of art. With thousands of sites to choose from, a fledgling artist might gravitate toward the obvious choices without looking into alternatives.

Etsy is a big-time player, and they will be around for many years to come, but they are far from the only solution. You can sell a lot on Etsy, but the challenge can be getting found in that massive marketplace. However, if you choose to use a different marketplace that may have less customers, but also less competition, you could corner a small segment of the market. The only way to find those nuggets online is to research, experiment, and adapt to new ways of thinking.

I also caution you to tread lightly into new markets because you do not want to get caught up in trying to be in too many places at once. You'll spend more time maintaining your different shops online, and less time making new products and sales. Balance is the key, and I encourage you to limit your choices to two or three outlets so you do not overextend yourself.

Speaking of balance, due to the proliferation of handmade goods both online and offline, and the popularity of local craft shows, it's easy to get wrapped up in the idea that the best place to sell your art is at street level. However, If you're looking to build a real art empire, you must consider diversification of your offerings, branch out to other arenas, and reach new customers.

You also should take into account how much time and effort it takes to manage a business that operates at craft shows. When calculating your expenses, it's important to remember that your time needs accounting. Sure, you could make back your booth fee, but you need to consider the time you spend ramping up, setting up, maintaining the booth, tearing down, and replenishing stock afterward. If you go in with an expectation of how much you need to sell in order to compensate for all that time, you will learn quick if art and craft shows are worth your while. Chances are, you could more effectively spend that time and energy promoting your work in your online shop instead.

WHICH SITES DO YOU CHOOSE?

I am as guilty as the next person when it comes to suffering from analysis paralysis over where to sell art. Maybe you have a few sites in mind, but don't know which to settle on. Perhaps you have no clue whatsoever and just need a push in one direction or another.

I've created this list with some of the more popular ways to get your art in the the hands of your admirers, breaking down the options into six main categories:

STOREFRONTS: The online equivalent to a brick-n-mortar shop, for the individual who prefers to be self-reliant.

MARKETPLACES: Sites that provide the complete infrastructure to operate your online business for a fee or commission.

DIRECT-TO-PRINT: Fully functional sites that take the work of selling, printing, and shipping your art out of your hands, giving you a small commission on each piece sold.

CURATORS: Sites operating like traditional galleries online, but with a wider reach, and sometimes on limited timelines.

COMMUNITIES: Social environments that expanded their influence to include opportunities for artists to sell.

STOCK IMAGERY: Providing images for other creators to use in projects of their own in a variety of ways.

Within each of those categories, we will discuss an array of sites that cover many segments of the digital art world.

My goal with this book is to give you a base—a list of go-to sites of various types, to expose you to the opportunities available. Not all of these sites will appeal to you and your style of art, but you might find at least one that you may not have considered.

HOLD UP THERE, HOT SHOT!

There's one thing you need to agree to before you read any further. The most important thing you can do for your art is to take action now. After you read through all these options, pick one, any one, and post up your work. It doesn't have to be the right choice, or your only choice, but make a choice. The time you wait before taking action is equivalent to the time until you reach that customer who has been waiting all their life to buy a piece of your work, but had no idea they wanted it until just that moment. Follow these tips for getting started, and you'll be off making sales in quick-like fashion.

1. Don't get bogged down in the details of things you feel you need to do before you post your work. You may think you need all the right materials and equipment to get your work done, but you do not. You can build up your studio over time, and your work will improve as you go, but instead of waiting for that moment to happen when you're *ready*, you could be making sales right now.

2. If you need photos taken, any camera will do right now, even the one on your phone. The composition of your shot is far more important than the quality of the camera you use to take it. Do

a little research on how the best shops are shooting their work, and try to emulate it (without outright copying) using the tools you already have. I know plenty of artists who take great photos with nothing more than an iPhone, and you can too.

3. Write some descriptive words about your piece; keep it short but tell a story. Until you can get better at creating the ultimate listing, with great SEO (search engine optimization) and appropriate keywords, the best thing you can do is help the people viewing your work understand where you were coming from when you produced it. They want to feel the art within you, not just know the details and features of the piece. Tell a good story, and it will resonate with them.

4. Take that photo and those words and post them up to a site today. Do not hesitate, do not stall—get it up there and be OK with the result. You can tweak later, but the important thing is to go through the process so you break through the fear of launching and know how easy it is to post something online. The next one will be even easier.

Getting that first piece up will be liberating, and you will feel like a rock star once it's done, but don't be dissuaded if it doesn't sell in an instant. The likelihood of it selling right away is small, but it will sell. Until then, go work on another piece, or another listing and repeat the process. As your shop grows, so will your revenue.

CHAPTER 2

STOREFRONTS

IF YOU BUILD IT THEY *MAY* COME

Operating your own online storefront is more time intensive than any other method for selling your work online because you are responsible for every aspect of the business. You create the work, add the listings, maintain the product, upkeep the site, do the marketing, and handle all the customer service. That said, storefronts can be the most rewarding, depending on your definition of reward. You will work hard maintaining your site and promoting yourself, but opposed to many of the other online options the largest chunk of profit stays in your pocket. If you're willing to put in the time and energy, a storefront will give you the best return on investment over time.

Additionally, there are numerous storefront options available beyond what I discuss here, but these few are the most prominent. I encourage you to research and build upon this information with a little web search to find more.

SHOPIFY

This is a new addition to the list, and although Shopify has been around awhile, it's only recently come up as a big player in the last couple years. In fact, I believe it's safe to say that Shopify is the new standard by which these other sites are measured.

When I asked a few friends about their Shopify experience, the general consensus about the site was that you could be a complete dummy with regards to web technology and still make a beautiful site quickly. Based on what I've seen from the user interface, it looks to be true. One of my good friends recently started her own Shopify account, and when I asked her why she decided to go that route, she said, "It's dumb enough even for me to set up," which is probably the strongest testimonial she could ever give.

What I like most about Shopify is the support they have available. There is a strong knowledge-base area, including a lot of detailed instructional videos, a customer forum, live chat and e-mail for difficult questions. If you need serious help, access to a list of Shopify experts who can help you design or manage your site from top to bottom.

It's easy to add products in their simple interface, as well as different types of pages, including a blog if that's what you want. Social media integration is simple, and from what I've seen, all of the Spotify templates are beautiful. If you don't want a cookie cutter design, there are third party templates you can buy, or you can hire someone from the experts group to design you something different.

Another cool feature that other storefronts haven't shown is Shopify's fully integrated point-of-sale setup. You can easily manage sales from an iPad, which is a cool feature if you have a brick and mortar store, or you are working an art show. Shopify takes it even further by supplying point-of-sale hardware that works with the system, like a cash drawer and a receipt printer.

The only downside to Shopify is the cost. The basic account is reasonable at $14 a month, but very limited. The standard starter option is $29 a month—not a lot of money, but when you're first ramping up your shop, it's something you might not invest in early on. The prices go steadily up from there, offering more services along the way, like extended stats and more third party integration, but I think the $29 level would suit most creative sellers well enough.

If you take into account all you get from Shopify for the price, it's hard to beat their option, and depending on what you sell, you only need to make a few sales a month to cover your costs.

BIG CARTEL

When it comes to servicing emerging artists and designers, Big Cartel used to have a sizable lead over the competition. Formerly the most popular of the storefront hubs, especially with artists and clothing designers, Big Cartel had an advantage over other sites based on the number of eyeballs they attract daily. Because they were the only player in the market for a long time, Big Cartel became top brand for its market, and people flocked to it for lack of any other options.

Of the artists I spoke with, everyone said Big Cartel doesn't do much to drive traffic to their shops. However, Big Cartel has a large and easy-to-navigate shop directory that helps potential buyers find new artists, not something you'll find at Shopify. If a customer is searching Big Cartel's directory and they want something similar to what you're selling, there's a good chance you'll be found, but they must actively seek out the directory first.

Big Cartel isn't the cheapest option, nor is it the most expensive way to do business. You can set up a free account to get started, but it's quite limited, only allowing for five products to be sold at a time. With the free account, you're stuck with a BigCartel.com URL instead of a custom web address, which is offered with the premium accounts. These paid accounts range from $10 to $30 a month and give a few more options as you step up in price. You also aren't committed to one level over another. Upgrading or downgrading is a relatively simple process.

If you're willing to put forth the effort to keep your shop fully maintained, and drive your own traffic to the site, perhaps Big Cartel, and its noteworthy name are the right fit for your business.

STORENVY

What Storenvy lacks in overall popularity to Big Cartel, it makes up for in pricing and features. Storenvy's marketplace is similar to Big Cartel, but with fewer shops in the list. However, they are growing fast, and are probably taking a decent amount of market from the bigger site. Like all storefronts, Storenvy doesn't do much to drive traffic to your shop unless customers are looking for you or your product. Some of your traffic will come organically, but most will need to come through your own promotional efforts.

The biggest selling point for Storenvy is the cost, as in they don't have any costs. If you have a product and want a website to sell it on, you can have a shop open in minutes without paying a dime. The limited upgrades of a dedicated URL and "special offers" functionality can be had for less than $10 a month—a smokin' deal, if you ask me.

From an outsider's point of view, it's hard to see what you get as far as stats like traffic data or demographics from these free accounts, but I'm willing to overlook those details if it means I don't have to pay a dime to get my store up and running. Although many shops don't take advantage of the capability, Storenvy is fully customizable, so you can design your shop to look however you'd like, in contrast to Big Cartel, which requires an upgraded account for the ability to customize your shop.

Another interesting selling point for Storenvy is the social media aspect, giving the community the ability to "like" or follow your page, which is immediately shared with their followers. I also like Storenvy's support system, and their helpful blog and newsletter. Even though I don't run a Storenvy site, their weekly newsletter brings good insight for anyone looking to sell online.

SELF-HOSTED SHOPPING CARTS

This is the scariest option for most folks starting out, and the most hands-on option I discuss here. With your own hosted website, you build the ship (or pay someone to build it to your specs), launch the ship, and man the helm all by yourself. The beauty of this approach is complete autonomy, not having to confine yourself to someone else's rules. The biggest downside to hosting your own site is the responsibility of all the upkeep and maintenance, which can be tedious for the experienced user and downright arduous if you're not tech savvy.

The costs to get started on your own site can be nominal, with some hosting accounts beginning around $4 a month. Upload a free or inexpensive content management system (CMS) to get yourself started and you could potentially have a website up and running in the course of an afternoon. However, the level of turnkey operation depends largely on what kind of site you're building.

When people ask me what they should do to get a site started, I advise them to begin with WordPress, the blogging platform turned CMS that is as robust as any high-priced system available on the market. WordPress can be relatively easy to get started for some, but there is a small learning curve in the beginning, especially if you've never hosted your own website before. That said, with WordPress installed, you can have a site up quickly, one with a plethora of free or cheap themes (templates) to use for your desired look and feel.

I mentioned that WordPress started out as a blogging platform, which it still is, but it's no longer essential to have a blog on your site with WordPress. Being a full-blown content management system, this means you're getting an easy-to-use system with an intuitive back-end to help you develop your site piece by piece. It's not perfect, but it's pretty close.

If you're looking to sell art through your shop, you'll need a shopping cart plugin for WordPress. Again, there are free and cheap options, like ZenCart, which is an adequate shopping cart solution, but its capabilities are limited. I personally have limited expertise with self-hosted shopping carts, so I advise you do plenty of research before committing to a system.

As with Shopify, Storenvy, and Big Cartel, having your own hosted shop means you will need to do all the promotion yourself, whether that's advertising, social media, or other marketing techniques. You'll have your hands full staying on top of all the site maintenance and still having time to create new products, so keep that in mind when making your decision.

GUMROAD

As the paths of innovation and independence converge, new technologies arise to help fill in the gaps when a segment of the market is not being fulfilled. Out of a need to provide a no-nonsense e-commerce solution for almost any website platform, and a frustration with the way merchant accounts like Paypal operated, services like Gumroad are becoming more popular.

With Gumroad, you add a product to your account, including photos, descriptions, and pricing, and it instantly becomes part of your storefront, but that's only the beginning. With a bit of code, or a Wordpress plugin, you can easily take that listing and share it on your site for people to buy directly from you. You ad a button, a widget, or a photo that links to the Gumroad listing, but instead of it taking people off your site, a small pop-up window allows them to finish their transaction right there on the page. Payments are processed immediately, and everything is SSL secured. There is no fee to join Gumroad, or to list your products. You only pay a 5 percent service charge on each transaction once someone purchases. As far as ease of use, there is nothing simpler. Gumroad is a great option for someone who wants to get products up on their site quick, but the service does have it's downfalls. First, it is better for someone who has only a few products. It's not good at inventory management, and shops with more than a few items will be frustrated with how you have to place snippets.

5 percent commission may not seem like much, but if you deal with high-end items like original paintings, that 5 percent adds up fast. Compared to Etsy, you still pay a commission to them, and to Paypal, but the difference being that Etsy drives traffic to your shop. Gumroad does not.

It is not a perfect option, but it is a decent option. I would recommend Gumroad to people who want to test e-commerce on their site before going bigger. It's best for those who have a few product or service offerings, or individuals who want a no muss, no fuss solution.

It may seem like I'm pushing you away from a self-hosted site, and perhaps I am for a majority of you. I do feel this option is the best for some shops, but for newbies it might not be the best way to start out. I recommend first-timers get their feet wet with one of the other storefront or marketplace options and see how that goes before committing to going solo.

CHAPTER 3

MARKETPLACES

PAY THE COST TO BE THE BOSS

Simply put, an online marketplace is a website that provides you everything you need to start selling, no matter how limited your resources, either at a monthly fee, or through per-transaction commissions.

It is advisable to consider the ups and downs of the marketplace route, the biggest upside being the rapid delivery to market. Even if you have only one piece of art to sell; as long as you have a photo, creative verbiage, and a merchant account like PayPal, you can start selling online with any of the options in this section. Also, because there are new players coming into the market, the competition creates innovation, and that innovation benefits both sellers and buyers. In the past, selling online was an convoluted mess; now there are options available that make it so all you need is to box up your product and ship it—all other aspects are handled online.

The biggest downside to marketplaces, arguably, are the fees that can stack up quick if you're not careful. I remember my first foray into selling on eBay years ago. Without paying enough attention to what I was posting, I quickly had a huge bill to pay, and not enough sales to cover the costs.

Pros and cons aside, marketplaces are where most people sell their work online these days because of the ease of use, and for a first-time seller, this is the recommended route to your first sale.

EBAY

Although I don't fully endorse this option any longer (I'll go into that more in a moment), I believe it's important to talk about eBay because they revolutionized how independent sellers of all types do business on the Internet. When it comes to online marketplaces for independent sellers, eBay is the king, far and away. Although I have limited experience selling art on eBay, I have sold plenty of other items there in the past. From what I have seen of other artists, eBay is a saturated market with lots of competition, and you risk getting overshadowed by more experienced and popular sellers.

When I asked a few artists I know who sell on eBay their thoughts, there was a resounding sigh and grumble about the site. In recent years, eBay has moved its focus away from the interests of its sellers and more toward the consumers. That's not necessarily a bad thing; consumers should have a lion's share of the influence, but eBay has made the space unbearable to a large segment of sellers.

Aside from the lack of seller support, the fees you can amass from attempting to sell on eBay can stack up quickly. Between fees for listings, fees for listing add-ons (bold headline, gallery photo, etc.), extended or reduced sales timelines, a percentage of every sale, for both eBay and Paypal, you can almost feel a hand in your pocket, sifting through your loose change.

On top of all that, many eBay consumers are not looking for high-quality art at a reasonable price. eBay buyers are more likely trying to find cut-rate art at a low price point, not caring about the quality over price. I imagine we all know someone who shops at both Walmart and Bloomingdales but they are the exception, not the rule. Most shoppers are either one or the other, and if eBay is the Walmart of the Internet, is that where you want your work sold?

It is important to note that even though eBay is the original marketplace, because of the lack of oversight on bootleg sellers from foreign countries, the environment is the wild west in comparison to newer, niche sites.

eBay is still the marketplace juggernaut, and an art listing here has the potential of hitting thousands, if not tens of thousands of more eyeballs than anywhere else. However, you must adequately weigh your expectations against these other factors. It couldn't hurt to try, and you might be successful, despite my warnings. Go into eBay slow and steady to make sure you don't lose more money than you can afford.

ETSY

If eBay is Goliath in the marketplace world, then Etsy is David, but this is the post–epic battle era, the giant is on his back and David stands victorious. The problem with defeating your nemesis is you run the risk of becoming like them.

I sold on Etsy for years, with reasonable success. I'm far from a super star like some, but I've sold enough to speak on the subject with authority. I feature artists from Etsy on *Fresh Rag* often and I openly confess my unabashed affection for the site, but Etsy is not without its own set of problems. No marketplace is going to be 100 percent perfect in your eyes or mine, but for any issues Etsy has, a multitude of positive things are happening at the same time.

Getting your items available for sale is easy, and it's almost scary-fast how quick you can be up and running—and indebted to Etsy—for a minimum of $0.20 (cost of a new listing).

Etsy is a marketplace geared toward handmade goods, art being a large portion of that population, and the staff at Etsy get what you're trying to do with your work. Their goal is to provide the best possible site to sell your goods to a world of people you may have never had a chance to sell to before now.

Most Etsy shoppers are savvy to the handmade ideal, know what they are looking for, and are willing to pay for quality work. I have done experiments with my prices in the past and can say with certainty that as long as you do not price yourself out of the market, people will pay the amount you ask. No one ever asked for me to sell them something cheaper than the listed price unless they were buying multiple pieces. If someone wants to buy multiples, then sure, they get a price break, but I still dictate the value to the customer and not the other way around.

Etsy also maintains a massive support community, a knowledge base both from Etsy staff and fellow sellers, waiting to be gleaned in order to make more sales. The community forums are extensive, and if you have a question, it has likely been asked and answered before. The Etsy blog is also filled with tons of information and inspiration. In fact, no other marketplace I know of puts as much time and energy into the support of its sellers … and buyers. Where eBay falters in social, Etsy excels in creating an adequate balance between the themselves, buyers, and sellers.

One of the biggest and best features of selling on Etsy is the impressive shop traffic. Etsy established itself at the top of the heap for handmade goods years ago, and people use Etsy as readily for handmade goods as they do Amazon for books or iTunes for music. Put your work up on Etsy and someone looking for work like yours is bound to find you. Etsy is also indexed by Google, so the traffic comes from external sources as well as internal. The internal search function is not perfect, but it's ever-evolving, and as it grows and improves, so will your shop as long as you do everything you can to make your shop better.

On the other side, Etsy can kill you slowly with fees if you're not careful. I have a friend who racks up fees in the hundreds of dollars every month, which scares her sometimes, but that means she is selling a lot of product.

Keep in mind your profit margin at all times. If you have a tight margin, you won't have as much flexibility, but once you know what you should charge, and what you're comfortable walking away with, it's easy to come up with a budget of how much to spend on listings, product quality, shipping, and fees.

ARTFIRE, CARGOH, MEYLAH AND MORE

My opinion of sites like Artfire, Cargoh, and Meylah is essentially the same for all three. All of them provide viable options for selling any type of creative work, each with its own personality. They each have things they do well, and some not so well, and even Etsy could take the occasional lesson from their competitors. Even if you were hosting your work on Etsy, there's no reason you couldn't do the same on these sites, or any other marketplace similar to them, of which there are many.

Two main detractors prevent me from using these sites: low traffic and lack of community. No other handmade marketplace can touch Etsy's traffic and search capability; there's just no two ways about it. Each of these sites have communities, but not nearly to the level of information and activity of the bigger site. In fact, it's not uncommon for people to discuss questions and issues about Artfire, Cargoh, or Meylah in the Etsy forums. That alone should give you all the information you need about which site dominates the marketplace world.

Each site is good in its own way, but I personally wouldn't use one as a standalone option. If I'm selling art on Etsy only, I may also use one of these others to post up some listings just in case there is a customer I could reach that I couldn't before. Just be mindful of the time involved in loading multiple listings to multiple sites with multiple fee structures. It could get expensive fast and you might spend more time maintaining your shop and less time creating.

ART FINDER AND SAATCHI

As the Internet expands, it continues to get more niche as time goes on. I would not be surprised if you told me by the year 2020 there would exist a site where someone can find nothing but abstract art on canvas created by North American artists over the age of 50—that's exactly how niche I expect the Internet to get in the future.

The more I talk with creatives, the more sites I find to feature, and over the last year, I've found a few marketplaces geared right at artists. Art Finder and Saatchi Art are a couple sites dedicated to serving the best original art and limited-edition art prints. I have not sold on these sites, but I reached out to a few individuals I know who have sold here, and they gave me the insider info to help you do the same.

The two sites are similar in that they are juried, taking in art that meets their qualifications. My artist friend, Amantha Tsaros says that it's not difficult to get accepted, but they are not afraid to turn away an artist who might not be at the caliber the sites like to showcase. Both sites feature a mix of established and emerging artists of all concentrations, including photography and sculpture.

Both sites do their own marketing, but expect the artists to do the heavy lifting when it comes to promoting themselves. Amantha finds that Art Finder does a better job of featuring her newest work when she uploads it to the site. She also told me she appreciated the level of customer service she gets on Art Finder compared to Saatchi. In fact, she tried to close her Saatchi account recently and found it difficult to make that happen without heavy coercion.

Other notable differences are that Saatchi is an American company and Art Finder is a European company, which means your customer base may end up being in different places. Also, there is a different pay system for both, so the frequency at which you are paid out is different.

One of the more peculiar differences is while Saatchi allows new users to browse art right away, Art Finder requires people to sign up first. This has a two-fold negative effect because not only can new people not see your work right away, but when you try to share a new listing, the people clicking through are led to a sign-in page instead of the listing itself. I find this one unusual, and considering the short attention spans of people online, I struggle to find the benefit in this approach.

The best part of being on a site like Saatchi or Art Finder is if you make the cut to sell there, it comes with a little bit more credibility than if you were selling on Etsy or other marketplace sites. Being seen amongst other artists who were also juried means you are worthy of a bit more consideration than the other schmucks who posted their amateurish work on eBay without any curation. If you think you can make the cut with your work, then give Art Finder or Saatchi a look.

In my opinion, Etsy is the clear winner in this segment because no other site will give you the flexibility to sell, the support of a strong community, and the reach of a site that is well over 30 million members strong. However, as with all categories in this book, you need to weigh your options against the focus of your work. Etsy is the leader, but it doesn't work for everyone. Know your product, know your customer, and know yourself, and then decide which site is best for you.

CHAPTER 4

DIRECT-TO-PRINT

FULFILLMENT IS FOR SUCKERS

As opposed to marketplaces and storefronts, where you are the source of all the materials being created and shipped, direct-to-print production houses like Zazzle, Society6, and Imagekind allow you to post up your art to be placed on various items or media. When ordered by a customer, the site produces the end product and ships it directly to the them. Once your art is on the site, it becomes a nearly hands-off situation for the artist. Sounds ideal, right? Perhaps, but there are a few things you need to consider before jumping in.

Successful artists on these sites claim that volume is the key. The more art you put up, and the better description you provide, the more likely you are to make sales. How much volume you need is undetermined, but I know from my own experience, it is more than a few. As soon as I had at least a couple dozen items up, my products started selling.

In exchange for the simplicity of not having to deal with production, your portion of the profit is slim. Rather than picking your own pricing and taking the majority of the profit from each sale, the DTP item has a base price, and you choose the percentage of revenue you want to gain over and above. Compared to selling your own work, with DTP, you will need to sell two or three items to equal the profit of one item you'd create yourself. Certainly, you could raise your percentage considerably to make up some of the difference, but you risk pricing yourself right out of the market.

Another point to consider is the quality of the products. Quality can be questionable at times, depending on which site you are working with. If you consider DTP as a viable option for your art, I recommend you buy a sample of your finished piece to see if it meets with your production standards, or if there is something you can do to improve the output. Perhaps the image comes out more saturated than you'd expected, prints with strange lines or artifacts, or the quality of the substrate is not up to your standards. You do not want to eat too much into your profits by purchasing multiple versions of your own prints, but going in with a reasonable perspective of the quality can only improve yours, and your customer's experience.

Finally, it's important to establish your identity from the start. Do you want to sell just art prints, or will you also promote your work on canvas? Maybe you want to expand to phone cases or laptop skins. Depending on which site you're using, the possibilities are endless. Go to Zazzle.com and you'll see a cornucopia of tchotchkes to embellish, but do you really want your art on some stranger's coffee mugs, neckties, or desk calendars? Finding the balance between idealistic artist and unscrupulous shill can be trickier than you expect. Do your research before making too big of a commitment.

Deciding which sites to put your work on can be tedious, but if you put the time in early it will be easier and more turnkey down the road. Since many of these sites are similar, I won't go into as much detail, but here is a snippet of what products each site offers.

ZAZZLE AND CAFE PRESS

These two sites are the kitchen sink of the direct-to-print world with tons of print options, and high traffic volume. Both sites allow you to put your work on a myriad of products, with Zazzle coming in at slightly fewer product types than Cafe Press, but better quality production. The themes tend to side more on popular memes or seasonal subjects, and shoppers are more inclined to buy for pop culture sake than for art. Of these two, Zazzle is my personal site of choice, and one where I've sold the most product.

Seeing competition from some of the other sites in this chapter, both of these sites have gone through site redesigns to a cleaner, more minimalist look, yet still similar to one another. Also, the new design of both sites attempts to take some of the steam off popular competitors, Red Bubble and Society6, which are more focused toward younger and hipper artists and designers.

The key to success on these sites is frequency and diversity. Because most shoppers are not looking for your particular shop on the site, but instead something that catches their interest, it's more important to be creating products that connect on themes. Graphic artists with a flair for typography or illustrators who like meme-based work will thrive here if they can pump out the work.

Many sellers on these sites make a decent income, some even full time income, but to do so, you must be vigilant. The more work you publish, the more likely you will be found in search. If you focus your energy toward trends, events, and seasons, you can hit on many levels. At the time of this writing, it is June, and across both sites, the summer theme is rampant. Holidays, sporting events, notable events like anniversaries and birthdays are all things that people seek out on Zazzle and Cafe Press. If making T-shirts and mugs about these subjects seems like fun, then wrap your hands around the latest meme and get to work.

IMAGEKIND

Originally only offering art-related substrates (prints, canvas, books), ImageKind was purchased by Cafe Press, and has since added mugs, calendars, mouse pads, and phone covers to their arsenal. My guess is that Cafe Press bought the site and reorganized it to compete directly with Society6 and Red Bubble, but in my opinion, not matching up quite as well.

Although Imagekind offers a unique service for getting your art prints made, they are by no means inexpensive. I have found more affordable options by going to my local office supply center with my own high-quality paper to get quality prints made, and canvas prints can be bought at Costco and for less.

Although Imagekind will give you a storefront to share and promote, if you wish to sell the art on your personal site, you could offer prints for sale, get each one printed as needed, and ship direct to the customer. This would obligate you to do the footwork, negating the purpose of a DTP product offering, but it is an option. Using Imagekind may not be the cheapest option, but at least you do not have to hustle around town getting the product made as each customer buys a print or canvas from your shop.

SOCIETY6 AND RED BUBBLE

In the first edition of this book, I lumped Red Bubble and Society6 together because they were similar in almost all respects. The sites looked the same, the artists featured where similar, and the products offered were identical. Since that time, both sites have created some competitive differentiation, but in subtle ways.

Both sites include hangable art with an emphasis on high quality imagery, as well as other products like mugs, phone cases, home goods, but now each site is shifting their individual focus. Where Society6 is geared toward artist and designer collaborations, Red Bubble emphasizes the different product offerings. Society6 still puts art prints at the forefront, while Red Bubble downplays the prints for the clothing and accessories. Society6 moved more toward pillows, rugs, and shower curtains while Red Bubble continues with tote bags and calendars.

The biggest difference I see between the two, is that Red Bubble has a link at the top of the site saying, "Sell Your Art," which shows me they want me to be a part of their offerings. Society6, on the other hand, has a somewhat elusive button at the bottom of the site that says, "Join Us," which doesn't tell me what they mean. Do they want me to be a customer or a seller?

I know that if you are going to sell on Society6, you must have your art available as an art print first. You cannot just make phone covers or T-shirts. They want your designs in an art print form, which proves the sites emphasis. If you were looking to be the next T-shirt design superstar without mucking up the works with other products, then perhaps Red Bubble might be your choice.

SPREADSHIRT

Last in line behind the rest, at least in popularity, Spreadshirt centers their business around clothing, but recently changed up their offerings to compete with the sites above by adding mugs, phone covers, and a few other incidental objects. In a digital world where the more niche you are, the more success you can find, I think it's unusual that Spreadshirt would try to compete head-on with the bigger players in the market. When you're successful at clothing, why move into buttons and pet accessories?

More competition in the market brings benefits and features for the consumer, but it also drives the smaller operations out of business because they can't compete with the bigger sites who operate on volume. I do not know Spreadshirt's circumstances, but I believe a focus on being the best purveyor of shirts or other clothing options would be a better approach for them. As it stands, I cannot see why anyone would choose them over their competition. I included Spreadshirt here to give you the option, but unless clothing is your main interest, I don't see this being the first choice for any artist.

ARTIST RISING AND FINE ART AMERICA

This section would be incomplete without these two sites, both functioning in similar ways to other direct-to-print sites, except focusing strictly on the market of art. Fine Art America is more popular in name with artists, but Artist Rising is gaining ground because of it's affiliation with Art.com, arguably the most popular art-oriented site on the web.

The biggest difference between these sites is in the types of product you can sell. Artist Rising is focused on selling open-edition prints, along with originals, but Fine Art America offers prints, posters, cards, phone cases, and original art. FAA also offers printing on different substrates, including paper, metal, and canvas.

From a design perspective, neither one of these sites makes a big impact in how they present the work, and in an era where people are viewing sites on mobile devices more than browser windows, these two sites do not stack up against any of the competition.

I do know a couple people who sell on FAA, none on Artist Rising, and although the sales are limited because of a lack of strong promotional efforts, the fact that artists can put up art there and have it sell without having to touch it after often makes it worthwhile for some passive income.

If I prescribe either of these sites, I lean toward Artist Rising for one reason: the site is the proving ground for Art.com, like a minor league of artists. If you sell well on Artist Rising, you could be brought up to the big leagues to Art.com, which is 100 percent exclusive. Once on Art.com, your chances of being promoted though the site, and selling big are a lot higher. I am unfamiliar with the vetting process of Art.com, so I cannot speak to how likely it is you will get there, but the possibility is available.

I am a big advocate of direct-to-print solutions for creatives, but it's not for everyone. I acknowledge that some will take issue with idea of "selling out" their work in order to make a quick buck. Truth be told, this process will never be a quick buck, but it can bring you some income with little effort after the actual art is created. You will not get rich, but if you are already creating art to be used and sold in other ways, why not look at these sites as a way to repurpose your work.

Also, when you go to many of these sites, you're going to find a lot of cheesy work, especially on Zazzle and Cafe Press, but do not let that dissuade you. The beauty of being an exceptional artist in a sea of mediocrity is that you can be a diamond in a coal mine. I recommend you go to these sites and do a search for work that resembles yours, either in style, or theme. You may find some decent artists in your search, but I guarantee you will find a lot of underwhelming art, and that alone should give you the motivation to push forward, because if those people can sell, why can't you?

CHAPTER 5

CURATORS

HANDPICKED FOR YOUR LIFESTYLE

Curated or juried websites such as 20×200, Fab, and 1xRUN are popping up all the time, and each one with a distinct style and methodology. From offering small-run, limited-edition art, to short-term "daily deals", a growing number of sites are looking to sell art fast and cheap. The upside is that they are constantly looking for new art to showcase, and even if you are an undiscovered talent, there may be a spot with your name on it.

Many of these sites are *new* in comparison to other sites we have discussed, and therefore hard to say what the downsides are to them in the long term, but I can imagine getting paid could be at the top of the list of concerns. Fulfillment of your product orders is another area to get squared away before committing to working with a curator site.

FIRE SALE ON ART

The daily deal group includes sites like Fab and Uncovet, which post several daily deals on a wide variety of art and design products. Since the last edition a lot has changed, specifically with Fab I'll explain later.

Though these sites are open to new work, they don't accept everyone; your work must be great and/or unique. You must also be able to handle the insane influx of orders that can come in a very short time. If you do get accepted, it's a quick way to sell a couple hundred pieces in a few days. Each site works differently, but essentially you are discounting your list price in exchange for selling in bulk. As with anything, make sure you know your profit margin because you could get stuck holding a very expensive bag if you get it wrong.

To become a featured seller you have to apply, and if they feel your product has the chops, they'll talk to you about how to best orchestrate the offering. Two things to keep in mind:

1. Do you have the ability to produce several hundred prints if need be?
2. Do you have enough margin to offer a good deal and make a profit?

WHEN THE FABULOUS FALTER

In 2012, Fab.com was on fire, the hot ticket for getting anything cool. They had a simple concept: three days to get your hands on some cool stuff. On day four, it was gone. This created a sense of urgency, and it wasn't uncommon for products to sell out. I remember one seller who sourced quilts made from traditional Indian Saris. The sale dropped, and within a few hours, 70 quilts were sold, each at $300 a pop. Fab saw the opportunity and immediately loaded up another 70 blankets. BOOM, they sold out again. They brought in one more round, and although they didn't sell out completely by the end of the three days, it was close. The seller made roughly $60,000 in three days. With sales happening like that on a regular basis, it would have been difficult for anyone to manage expectations.

Fab saw the money, and they went after it. Within a year, their entire business model changed. Instead of three days, some went up to five days. Instead of sending out one email a day, you could potentially get several messages, featuring a different category of design. Before long, customers stopped getting interested. Before, there was a limited supply on cool design products. After, there was a glut of products, and the attention span of the customers waned. Fab also found itself in a quagmire of taking any kind of product if they thought it could sell.

Sometime in 2013, Fab realized they were headed down the wrong path. They needed massive change in order to keep going. They laid off 100-plus employees, shifted their point of view, and changed the business model completely. Technically you can't call Fab a daily deal site any longer. The best way to describe them now would be an online store that puts customer service first—the Zappos of design products. They brought all the products in-house, did all the shipping themselves, and instead of customers missing out on deal deadlines, the items are always available, at least until they run out.

Fab is trying to pivot their business, but I believe it is too late. They have lost their glimmer, and although they're not going anywhere right away, I do believe they will never capture the magic they once had when design was good and exclusivity created need.

Daily deal sites are great for getting your name out to a bunch of new customers who might normally never find your work, but not the best at cultivating return customers to your shop. Additionally, the people on these sites are buyers looking for something new and cool to buy. With a wide audience base, you're bound to find your ideal client. All types of items sell on these sites at wildly different price points. As long as your work is good and you have a proven record of selling, the sites do their best to accommodate you. Just be very clear with yourself about what you need to make out of the deal for it to be worth your while financially.

MEMBERSHIP HAS ITS PRIVILEGES

The sites in what I call the *exclusive curation* group operate more online galleries than marketplaces. The sites here are only a few examples, and each have their certain types of art they look to feature.

Of course, each site has its own identity, as well as a specific way it offers the art for sale, but the common thread is a focus on limited-edition prints offered either for a set period of time (days or weeks), or for as long as the limited run prints are available. Some sell faster than others, and sometimes slow movers end up discounted until they are liquidated.

This group comes with the biggest barrier to entry over any other options mentioned thus far. Some of these sites are not actively taking new artist submissions, but that does not mean you should not try if you feel this is where you belong. I believe, if this is your desired market, then go after it, but go in with low expectations. Also, if you do make it into one of these sites, no one is getting rich, except maybe the sites themselves. I still recommend you spread your love around to other sites for more saturation.

20×200 AND MAMMOTH & CO

These two are similar sites, offering a wide variety of art, in several sizes per print. The popularity of the artist tends to dictate the amount of prints offered in a particular print run, but pricing tends to be universal, varying only slightly on special occasions. For the consumer, these sites are a great way to start a small art collection at a reasonable price.

20x200 tends to showcase photographers more often than painters or illustrators, but there are plenty of traditional artists featured. Mammoth is almost the opposite, with more emphasis on illustration and fine art.

1XRUN

1xRUN is unique in that it's a combination of both a daily deal and an exclusive curation site. Once or twice a week, a new piece is offered, and the runs are extremely limited. Pricing is moderate to expensive, depending on the popularity of the artist, but some well-known names are popping up on a regular basis. 1xRUN is the most exclusive site of this group, with no mentions anywhere about artist submissions. 1xRUN curators hand-pick all their featured artists, but again, that doesn't mean you don't have what it takes to be there; you just have to get yourself noticed. Street and subculture art is their mainstay, but they also feature illustration and design prints on occasion.

PAPIRMASSE

This site operates a bit different from the others because you're buying into an art subscription rather than individual pieces. Think of it as *art-of-the-month* club. You pay a flat amount, no matter when you sign up, and you get a new, small print in the mail every month for the duration of your subscription. There is no mention of limited-edition here, and the size and shape can range from piece to piece, as does the quality of the paper, so it's possible the art is printed on traditional card stock or something similar. Based on the crazy-cheap pricing of $5 a month, my guess is Papirmasse is contracting an artist to do a particular piece with the intent of producing enough prints to make the deal financially viable for them, which could mean large open-edition runs.

SERGEANT PAPER AND COGO HOUSE

I dig these two European alternatives, first because of their product offerings, but also from their marketing. I really wish I could read French because Sergeant Paper has one of the best newsletters around, and I'm dying to know what they are saying. Cogo House is no slouch either, but I lean more toward the work at Sergeant.

Being in the United States, as an artist, I personally would not think to focus my attention toward these sites, but I have had dozens of European customers over the years, so selling on sites outside our normal circle of influence might garner us a following far beyond what we can imagine.

Use your time and energy wisely, but if you're reading this from abroad, or you happen to speak the language, give these sites a whirl.

Each of these curation sites will take considerably more time and effort to be part of than anything we discussed up until now, but with a little energy, tenacity, and will, you could manage some serious success. If you're fresh out the gate with your prints, you likely won't get featured on any of these sites right away, but that shouldn't stop you from trying. If you feel your work fits the model of any of these sites, I encourage you to pursue them until they either accept you or tell you to go away. And if they say no, there are a lot more sites to choose from.

The amount of work you put into your own self-promotion before getting noticed by these sites is key. Gather a small army of fans, sell some of your art in different places, and you might gain the attention of these exclusive sites. The important point is to keep trying until you find the market you want to be in most and rock it 'til it's dead.

The important lesson is that daily deal sites are a trend, and like most trends, they eventually die out. I am keeping this section in the book because they still serve a place in the list, but their pull is not as strong as it was at their peak.

CHAPTER 6

COMMUNITIES

TAKE SOCIALIZING TO A NEW LEVEL

There are a bazillion art and design-related communities online—too many to mention in a lifetime, let alone in the confines of this chapter. For the consideration of both your time and mine, let's discuss the few I have personal experience using.

Many of the sites I've discussed in previous chapters have community efforts that act as a support system for their thousands of members (Etsy, Zazzle, Storenvy), but that's not their main focus. By contrast, DeviantArt, Gigposters, and Behance are communities first, portfolio hosts second, and everything else after that. You can sell your work on these sites, and each one approaches that task differently, but selling is a secondary aspect to what they offer in total.

THE KEY WORD IS DEVIANT

You might not know this, but DeviantArt.com is the largest social media site for artists by a large margin. In fact, it wasn't too many years ago that DeviantArt had more active users than Facebook, Twitter, Myspace combined. Let me say that again just to be clear: A site dedicated to art was, for a time, the largest social media site on the Internet, yet still, many people have never heard of it.

Of course Twitter, Facebook, and Instagram have grown exponentially in the last few years, and they're not looking back anytime soon, but it's an amazing feat that a niche art forum could command so much traffic. The downside to a large community? As an artist, you enter as a tiny fish in a big ocean, but like any social media sites, you can create your own ecosystem.

DeviantArt has not changed its look and feel for many years. The layout you see today is almost identical to what it was 10 years ago, and although the community is large, I don't see them making major changes anytime soon.

Another downside to having so many users is that it can be difficult to separate the wheat from the chaff. There's a lot of junk on DeviantArt, mostly young kids looking to kick off their artistic careers, or fanboys who draw a hundred pictures of Dragonball Z characters. Your work may be exceptional, but it can get lost with all the other junk floating around on top. Staying prominent and popular on the site requires effort, but we're not here to talk about your social skills.

The process for selling your art on DeviantArt is essentially the same with direct-to-print sites. You supply the art, pick the price point (above the "wholesale" pricing), and the site does the rest. It's easy and painless, but as I warned with other production houses, make sure you know what you're selling. The quality of the product may not be up to your standards, so do your research.

Also, I have tried putting up items for sale to test this arena, but I never put my energy into building my network. I think if you are going to be successful selling on DeviantArt, you need to invest in the community, which is true for most sites, but you need to ask yourself if the time spent is worthwhile—sales will surely dictate.

BOYS TOWN IS FILLED WITH POSTERS

As a constant source of inspiration, and simultaneous consternation, GigPosters delivers. No other site on the Internet satisfies my craving for cool design and illustration work quite like GigPosters. However, it never fails to make me realize how much I suck in comparison to some of the talented folks on this site. With heavy hitters like Jay Ryan, Aesthetic Apparatus, and the ubiquitous Frank Kozik hanging around, it's easy to get intimidated.

Aside from a large database of poster designs you can search through, Gigposters has a massive community forum. Years ago, this was the first art-related forum I participated in, and I wasn't even designing posters at the time. I loved poster design so much, I wanted to hang out with the cool kids. The problem with calling them the cool kids is that a lot of them believe it. The forums can be a bit heavy in trolls, thriving on the blood and bones of newbs, but if you have thick skin, can take a few licks, and do more reading than speaking, you'll be OK.

It can be hard to avoid the trolls; the scene seems to generate a bit of the "I'm cooler than thou" snarkiness because tons of fresh-faced designers are always sucking up to the cool kids. It's been years since I visited the forums, but I check in every once in awhile, and the same snarky attitude seems to come up, just with different individuals.

That said, for every troll on the forums, a dozen or more kind and courteous folks are more than willing to help out the new guys. There's a ton of information to be had on those forums, you will be wiser for spending time there. Just mind your attitude, or risk a virtual beheading.

On the selling tip, the Gigposters online shop operates like a marketplace. Similar to selling on Etsy, you pay Gigposters a small amount for the listing, keep the cash from the sale, and do all the fulfillment yourself. The only difference is you're marketing directly to a very specific niche of collectors. You can sell more than art prints here, like T-shirts or original art pieces, but the lion's share of products sold are posters and prints.

Also, although I have seen digital and offset* printed posters sold here, those are few and far between. Screen printed posters are the norm, as they are throughout the site, so don't be shocked if the prints you made from your Canon desktop printer don't go over well with this group—I speak from experience.

LIKE LINKEDIN FOR CREATIVE TYPES

I learned something very interesting about Behance. The founder, Scott Belsky, used to be a heavy hitter at Goldman Sachs. How does a man working for the most prominent (and infamous) investment firm go off to start a social arena for creatives? It's a head-scratcher to say the least, but he's done a good job with the site, so I assume he has only the best of intentions.

Behance is on the opposite side of the spectrum from most art communities. If DeviantArt is the neighborhood pool, Behance is the athletic club. I don't mean to imply Behance is exclusive, because it's not, but the people there are in a more serious mindset. If you're on Behance, you're not just hanging out, but on a mission to further your career. You're showcasing your portfolio in the best possible manner, looking to interact and find work, or trying to hire someone for a project.

The structure of the social community is similar to DeviantArt in that most interaction comes from "likes" and comments on your submitted work. They do not have forums like Gigposters, and there is no massive knowledge base to tap into, making this the weakest of the three sites from a social setting, but I believe that is by design. It would seem the intention of Behance is less about interacting and more about getting work done, implied explicitly if you read the founder's book, *Making Ideas Happen*.

Selling on Behance is completely different from the others in that you don't sell anything on Behance. Instead, you link up to whatever other site you're selling through (Etsy, Society6, Big Cartel, etc.) and Behance simply sends the customer over to that site for the transaction. I personally think it's a missed opportunity for Behance, but nobody who worked at Goldman Sachs ever gave up a dime on purpose, so I'm sure they are getting referral commissions.

For the sake of selling success, I personally would never use these forums as my main selling opportunity. Gigposters used to be the place to go for screen-printed posters, but with the rise of Etsy, many of those artists have taken their work to the handmade juggernaut. These sites are great for support, both for its knowledge base and notoriety, but selling here should serve as secondary options to your main source. Use the communities for their strengths, and then focus your strengths on the sites that sell better for your work.

*Offset printing is a standard printing process that uses a four-color system on large print presses, typically for marketing materials, packaging, movie posters, or other mass-produced print projects.

CHAPTER 7

STOCK IMAGERY / DOWNLOADABLES

IF "HANDS OFF" IS YOUR MOTTO ...
Then this chapter is for you.

Originally, I did not want to include this chapter because it focuses almost exclusively on designers and illustrators as opposed to artists who sell prints or originals. As I thought about it deeper, the point of the book is to give you all the options available for sharing your work in different ways, so it made the cut.

I know that many of you come from different concentrations, like myself. I'm an artists at heart, but a graphic designer by trade. I can focus my energy in different ways, sharing my work with different customers, spreading the love, and bringing in income from a variety of sources. Some will shrug off this section because they believe stock imagery to be the bastardization of art. Many photographers have given me an earful of opinions about why stock imagery is bad for the business, same with illustrators and designers. If you feel the same, then this section is not meant for you. Go ahead and jump to the next chapter while the rest of us talk about extending our brand.

For those who know little or nothing about stock imagery and downloadables, the idea is simple: you create art, illustrations, or photos to be used over and over again by people who wish to use the work in something they are creating, either professionally or for themselves. As an art director, I have used stock imagery many times, either for photo images as the center of a campaign, or illustrations to finish off a piece. I have also used stock imagery in some of my digital collage pieces when I could not physically take the photo myself.

The reason some consider stock imagery the work of the devil is because of the low price point that the art is sold. You can buy a high-resolution image on iStockphoto for around $10, only a portion of which goes to the artist, and to some, that is a travesty. However, they do not see the big picture, and potential. The photographer may only earn a portion, but he can earn that over and over again. Although most artists on these sites make little to no money, there are many who make a nice living from their work. Like anything else, it's the ones who put in the work who get the most reward; they make their own luck.

The beauty of stock imagery will always be its ability to generate income without having to touch the file after it is uploaded. Will you be removed from the customer service side completely? Not likely, but a lot of what happens to the file after you post it up becomes the responsibility of the site administrators, which is also why the percentage of payout to the artist can be low. If you appreciate the ability to post up and move on, similar to direct-to-print, this segment is all you, all day long.

The barrier to entry on these sites can be difficult. They are flooded with new artist requests daily, and the sites must be careful to only showcase the best possible work, rejecting substandard art on a regular basis. If you want to work here, you better have your chops up, and be prepared to work your butt off if you want to be successful.

There are dozens, if not hundreds of stock photo sites, but the following are the ones I have used the most often, all for various reasons.

ISTOCKPHOTO AND SHUTTERSTOCK

In the beginning of the stock photo world, there existed sites that allowed you to buy rights managed and royalty free stock, but all of it at a premium price. In 2000, iStockphoto was born, and originally was dedicated to offering free stock images. The quality was low, but they were free. Shortly after, the company started charging for the images, and they were profitable from the start. There success was born on the idea that you could get quality imagery at a very low cost. Normally, a royalty free image would cost you around $50, depending on who you bought it from. iStockphoto charged $10, and immediately caught fire.

For years, I used iStockphoto exclusively, but I never liked their purchasing model. You couldn't buy just one photo. You had to buy a packet of credits at different price points; the more credits you bought, the better the price. However, it often left me with extra credits at the end, and I would need to buy more credits to fill the gap.

Sometime later, Shutterstock came into popularity, challenging iStockphoto for stock image supremacy. At first, the quality wasn't quite the same, but has since gone up, and the way they differentiate themselves from their bigger competitor is to offer the ability to buy per image credits. They also were the first to start subscriptions, where you paid a flat monthly fee, and could download up to a certain amount of images per day or per month. iStockphoto soon followed their lead, and it's now become the way many of their customers by stock.

If you're an traditional artist, and you want to sell your work as stock imagery, you need to be savvy with creating art that works for that purpose. You also need to be able to output your art in the file formats required. If you don't have a copy of Photoshop or Illustrator, get one right away, or some equivalent.

If you're a photographer, illustrator, or graphic artist, before you start sending your work to these sites, make sure you know their submission guidelines. Because a lot of imagery is based on trends or seasons, these sites will get overloaded with those types of images. If it's the holiday season, they are less likely to approve your Christmas tree art because they probably got 100 designs submitted that day with the same concept. That doesn't mean you shouldn't submit your Christmas tree, but make sure it is unique in a way that it sets itself apart, and also appealing enough for the site to consider it commercial.

These sites regularly update their guidelines, and they will tell you what kind of work they are looking for. More importantly, they will tell you what kind of work they do not want to see. Take care in that some of your work will get rejected, but they will give you a hint as to why. If it's a subject matter, then hold that one off for another time. If it's quality, then go back to the drawing board and clean it up.

You could also feasibly put your work up in both places, but both sites offer a higher payout for artists who keep their work exclusive. That doesn't mean you can't be in both places, but perhaps you keep certain pieces in one spot, and a different set in others.

The way you get paid works on a sliding scale. The more you sell, the higher you get paid. Someone who sells 200 pieces a month is going to get paid exponentially more than someone who sells 100 pieces a month. iStockphoto's royalty schedule is based strictly on how many credits you've had redeemed over your lifetime. Shutterstock is a bit harder to work out, but overall, more generous to the artist.

As I said in the beginning, there many sites in this category, and these two are just the top contenders. You could put your art in a few different places and make residual, passive income from a variety of sources, but you will need to put the work in to make it worthwhile.

ENVATO

Easily the most robust of all the sites in this section, Envato is a marketplace for several types of downloadables. They have many subsites, each dedicated to a specific niche, including website themes, plugins and code, video, audio, 3-D files, and for our benefit, graphics and photos.

GraphicRiver and PhotoDune not only offer stock imagery as an option, but they also sell templates, actions, and scripts that can be used in your work. Want to get that neat flaming effect on your image that you saw in a magazine recently? It's probably on PhotoDune. If you're a wizard in Illustrator or Photoshop and have a few actions that you use that you think others could benefit from, then you could sell them on these sites. Overall, Envato is more B2B—designers selling to other designers, which strengthens their community.

Of course, you can sell your graphic and photo stock, but that's only a small portion of what these sites offer. That brings up a good point; these sites are small in comparison to iStockphoto and Shutterstock—like head of a pin small, but the the core users are devoted to Envato.

The biggest upside to Envato is the payout. An exclusive artist makes a minimum of 50 percent of the payout, all the way up to 70 percent, which is unheard of at the bigger sites. Even nonexclusive contributors make 33 percent, which is still higher than Shutterstock and iStockphoto. Your volume may be lower with Envato, but at least you know they are looking out for you as a creator.

Envato also has a strong community and forums. The more I dig into Envato, the more impressed with their dedication to the creators. Most of their focus goes toward developers and software engineers, but overall, they want to make sure their "authors" are represented and treated well.

INKD

For anyone who isn't a graphic artist or illustrator, you may want to skip this one. Inkd serves one very small segment, and they do it well: branding and collateral. If you're a logo designer, or know how to create epic design templates for print projects, then Inkd might be what you need.

Their core business is logo design at a discount. They sold prefab logo designs in the past, but changed their model to custom design only. I cannot tell if any designer is allowed to contribute to the logo designs, so I won't talk about that portion, but if you can make interesting templates for business cards, letterhead, flyers, and data sheets, why not put it up on the site for others to use?

Competition, visibility, and a lack of success stories might be good reasons to not consider Inkd. There's some strong work on the site, but I don't know anyone who sells here, and I rarely see Inkd's presence online. Being one of the only places I know online that sells this type of work, and with a solid portfolio to showcase, I think Inkd should pour their energy into boosting the site's awareness, but that's an outsider's opinion.

Their payout percentage is relatively low at 20 percent. Granted, iStockphoto is less overall, but what you lack in payout there, you gain in volume because iStockphoto is massive in comparison to Inkd. It strikes me as opportunistic, but that's one man's opinion. You may find that your work shines there and you could kill it with passive income from people buying your postcard layouts.

ETSY

Wait, how does Etsy get two mentions in one book? Because change happens, and in June of 2013, Etsy made a major change to how people sell downloadables. Before 2013, people could sell their stock imagery on Etsy, but once a customer bought something from your shop, you had to physically serve that file to them through e-mail or other means.

Now Etsy has instant download capability. When someone buys from you, they get a link to the file, and that link is always available to them. Not only is this good for the customer, but it's also good for you since it takes one aspect of customer service out of your hands. You no longer need to answer inquiries from customers who didn't get the file and you need to resend—it's now in their account history for them to access.

Another great thing about selling downloadables on Etsy is that it doesn't matter what you sell, it's all good ... within reason, of course. I've seen people sell everything from digital scrapbook papers to photo frame templates. You can buy printables for kid's parties, or vector graphics to use in your own art.

Some of you may have even bought this book through my Etsy shop as a downloadable PDF. If you did, thank you for being part of that experiment. I intend on selling all my future books in this genre through Etsy, because why not?

The biggest upside to selling downloadables through Etsy is the revenue. Your cut is huge in comparison to all the other sites in this list. At $0.20 a listing plus selling percentage fee, how can you beat that payout?

Combine the payout with the reach of Etsy and you can make a killing. If you look at the top 10 artists in the graphic design area of Etsy, each of them is making a healthy income from their downloadables, and that's only one segment. My illustrator friend John W. Golden recently launched an Etsy tagging guide. In less than a week, he sold 50 copies. He never intended it to be an income generator, more for helping other artists on Etsy, but it's safe to say he made a good choice.

Downloadables may not be your thing, but as the market grows for people doing their own DIY products, there's more opportunity for creative individuals to make money sharing their talents with others through digital files.

    The key to success in this market is a combination of tenacious pursuit of quality, and a strong marketing effort. We call it passive income, but once you start selling on stock image sites, you will find that there is nothing passive about it. Work is work, even if you don't have to put your hands on the product after it's made. One thing I notice from the top sellers in any market is that volume almost always equates to sales momentum. The more products you have up, the better your overall sales will be, but if you rest on your piles of money, you risk stagnation. You need to keep the stock fresh in order to remain relevant.

CHAPTER 8

WIDER REACH AND BIGGER SALES

Now that you are armed with all this knowledge on different sites to showcase your work, the question remains, what do you sell? Sure, you could sell your one piece of art, or one photograph, or one design to one customer at a time, but is that really the best use of your time and talent?

Consider for a moment that your art could be repurposed many different ways to help you generate more content, more fans, and more sales. Instead of doing one piece of art at a time for one customer at a time, you do one piece of art for lots of different customers and sales. If you believe in the idea of residual income, keep the following thoughts in mind.

ALL POSSIBILITIES SHOULD BE CONSIDERED

This section is all about spitballing ideas, not hardline rules to live by. What one artist does with their time and energy might not work for another. Before you consider any shifts in your sales or promotion strategy, it is a good idea to examine your situation and make a judgment call on what works best for you. That said, there's a strong chance what you are capable of achieving far exceeds your predisposed comfort level. Do not let misguided fear and self doubt keep you from success. Stop selling yourself short—be fearless!

THERE ARE NO SELLOUTS

If one artist calls another artist a sellout for achieving some financial success, the haters are likely hacks who can't cut it with the business side of art. That's harsh, but in many cases, true. If you list your art at various places, and it sells, this does not make you a sellout, but a creative business owner.

In no other area except art is lack of success considered the ideal path. My theory is that at one point in history, a couple of unsuccessful artists were sitting in a cafe, drinking coffee and eating baguettes (because they couldn't afford anything else), talking about not being able to sell art. Suddenly one says to the other that their art is too profound for people to understand, and that is why it does not sell. Soon enough, they are cheering each other on to celebrate their individuality and declaring that not selling art was the purist pursuit of artistic expression, and anyone who did sell art was a sellout. I can imagine them heckling artists who were featured in fine galleries and museums, calling them shills and puppets of the establishment. Soon, those artists shared their thoughts with other artist friends who couldn't sell their art, and eventually they justified their starving artist revolution,which has perpetuated ever since.

I already know that is not you, because you wouldn't have bought this book if it was, but you may know people who feel this way about art, and they might heckle and harass you for being entrepreneurial. Let them heckle. While they're eating baguettes, you and I will go out for steaks.

DO NOT FEAR COMPETITION

Even if you create the same type of product or process as the artist next to you, you are not them, and they aren't you. If you have ever taken a life drawing class, this should be obvious; everyone draws the same naked, old guy, but no two penises look the same. You may create a similar product or service as another artist, but you will always add your unique style to it, and that style is why your customers love you and your work and not the other guy.

MARKETING IS FUNDAMENTAL

Crafting a piece of art is only the first link in a long chain of creating new content and more opportunity for sales. Although what we're talking about in this book is where to sell your art, creating content from your art is another way to promote your work and attract more sales.

What starts as paint to canvas or clicks of a mouse to a digital image, can lead to content as videos, blog posts, training tools, or other derivative art, which could lead to new customers.

Using a traditional painting as an example, I'll run through the possibilities of things that can be created from one canvas. However, these concepts extend far beyond traditional art. Any creative individual reading this can adapt these techniques for greater reach and sales.

IT STARTS WITH A SINGLE BRUSH STROKE

Before you place a single dab of paint on a canvas, consider setting up your video camera, digital SLR, and/or camera phone, and get set to record the process. Since you're doing the work anyway, might as well document it.

Some artists will take photos of them at work. Others will video tape the entire event until completion. You can use those photos and videos as content on your blog and social media, and then carry them over to the various art sites as process shots to engage the viewer, spreading your creative expression all over the Internet. I'll break down some options here for you and that should get your brain cooking for different ways to share the love.

SHARING ON SOCIAL MEDIA

You may not be able to quantify money made from social media efforts, but you can gain a lot more followers, fans, and potential customers through these sites, creating evangelists for your brand. That said, it's essential to balance your time on each social platform so you're not eating into your profits by spending all your time on Facebook, Twitter, Instagram, and Pinterest.

Instead, develop a process that you can sustain easily, will not take much time, but gives you the maximum amount of exposure. The following is my proven process for growing my followers and customers. There are certain aspects you want to keep consistent, and others that are flexible, so try this method for a bit and tweak as you see fit.

To make relating to these sites easier, I rank them into two levels: primary and secondary. YouTube and Instagram are primary because they are the source location for your video and images. We use these sites to feed to our secondary sites like Facebook, Twitter, and Pinterest, as well as your blog and e-mail newsletter, if you have one. If you don't have an e-mail list, get one! At the end of the pipeline will be your shop listing, if that is the desired result.

This pipeline technique should not be confused with a sales funnel, which is about leading people through your products in hopes of up-selling them. I talk more about sales funnel in a bit, but it's important to know that these are separate and essential marketing techniques to implement.

This is a good time to mention that all of your efforts should be with a goal in mind. Maybe that goal is to get them to your shop, get them to your blog so you can have them join the e-mail list, or you just want to engage fans with cool pics and videos. Whatever that goal is, make sure you are clear on it and you provide people the opportunity to interact by giving a call to action. Do not be afraid to say, "Check out our site for some of our best products," "Sign up for our newsletter for special deals," or, "I have a question for you. Come over and let me know what you think about…"Yes, this is thinking like a marketer, or a salesperson, but now is the time to put the big-kid pants on and treat your business like a business. You can be friends with your people and still be a business owner.

Many customers have been lost by artists because they were too timid to ask for the sale. Your customers want to be asked; they want to be told how to get more of you. You can give a call to action without being slimy or salesy, and if you provide value, the customers will come running.

TEASE, TAG, AND TELL

Whenever I post to Instagram, I like to use what I refer to as the 3-T method of Tease, Tag, and Tell to entice and encourage sharing. This is how it works.

TEASE - Often when posting a photo, I allude to something bigger. If I shoot a photo of my work, perhaps I show it as a work in progress, only show a portion of the finished product, or I show it at a distance so it makes people want to see more. I also like to give subtle hints about the image and what it might lead to if they follow the breadcrumbs to my site. Dangle the carrot a bit, keep them enticed, but remember to give them the carrot at some point. Tease them too much and they will bail on you.

TAG - Using tags in my image description helps me in a couple ways. First, it helps draw attention from people on Instagram that I might not have reached before. If I tag my image as #art or #design or something relating to the image, then people searching at random for that tag could stumble across my image, "like" it, and maybe become a new fan.

Also, when I share that image and description to the secondary sites, those tags will come across. Now that Facebook is supporting tags, all of the major secondary sites have the residual effect of bringing in new potential fans, just as I did in Instagram to start.

Tags can be touchy for some. In Instagram, it's perfectly OK to load up your tags, the nature of how people operate on that platform. In Twitter, space is limited, so tags are used sparsely to avoid clutter. Although Facebook allows tags, they are still a foreign object in that space, and too many tags would turn people off. In short, use discretion.

One small technique I've tried with success is to upload my image with a basic description, maybe a tag or two, and then send off to the far reaches of the social universe. Then, go back and comment right away on my photo with some additional tags. Those tags will only be attached to Instagram, and won't bother people elsewhere.

TELL - Plain and simple, share that image everywhere. Sometimes I will send the image direct from Instagram to Facebook, Twitter, Pinterest, and Tumblr. Other times I will post it to my blog first, build a story around it, and then send it out to the secondary sites. The goal is to lead them back to your blog and/or shop as often as possible.

If you're not keen on sending that photo to the different sites all at one time, then send to one or two at first, then later, go back and share in the others. That way you're spreading it around over time, and not annoying those who follow you on all your accounts.

QUOTES ARE KILLER

People love inspirational quotes, almost to a fault. Really, who doesn't? A small snippet of wisdom handed over by someone smarter than me, I'll take that all day long. People love them even more when they can share a good quote across their different social media platforms. Let's be honest, they share it because it makes them look smart or profound, and ego is a great motivator.

You just took a photo of your work; perhaps that photo could make a good background for a poignant quote. Paste the text onto the image (can be doing with a variety of apps), then share and tag just like you would any other image. Quotes are huge on Facebook and Instagram, even more so on Pinterest and Tumblr. Use those visual mediums to your advantage to inspire and attract people.

RESHARING

The beauty of Instagram is that they can have the added benefit of bookending the process. You share a photo from Instagram to your blog and your Facebook page. Then grab a screenshot of your site and share it back on Instagram again, for instance, showing people that the new piece is up on your shop, or if you hit a milestone on social media, "I just hit 1,999 fans. Who will be #2,000?"

This is not something you want to do too often for fear of sharing things that do not relate to the group you're speaking to. If you do try this technique, make sure what you are sharing is interesting enough to post a second time around.

VIDEO KILLED THE TEXT-ONLY BLOGGING STAR

In this world of ever-increasing better, faster, bigger, more, it's no wonder that video has become the king of all content. Since the 1950s, we've strapped our eyeballs to animated screens for entertainment. Now that it's easier to produce videos and more common to spend hours on YouTube, it's a wonder that you're not already on there sharing your story.

If you did shoot that video of your process, now is a good time to take stock and see what you can produce from it. Depending on the length, you can turn that video into a variety of helpful tools.

You may have seen time-lapse videos of artists on YouTube; a long video sped up to show an entire piece painted over a period of a couple of minutes instead of hours or days. As an artist, I love watching these, especially if it gives me a chance to see how the artist does what they do, like a studio insider.

If a video is on the longer side, you can break it up into a few different videos, share it over a period of days or weeks, and create a buzz around your posts. One of my clients uses this technique, and does a great job of engaging the viewer with some intro video of her discussing the process, narrating over the time-lapse, and then closing it out with more of her at the end.

Once you have a few videos under your belt, you can share the series in one blog post, like a mini training series. Or you could collect several from different artists compiling them for variety. Spreading the love around to other videos in one post could get you some notoriety from those other artists, and maybe their fans.

Going a step further, let's say you made an instructional video, documented your whole process of doing the painting, or maybe you did a "from easel to market" video series, but instead of giving it away for free, you sold it as a course on your own site.

ENOUGH CONTENT. WHERE'S THE MONEY?

OK, so you've blogged and YouTubed and Facebooked yourself silly, and you have lots of new followers to show for it, but how does that equate to dollar bills? The basic math says the more eyeballs on your work, the more sales you'll make. You may have a buyer for your latest piece, but that only means one sale, and once it's gone, it's gone. If you're selling your pieces at a premium price point, perhaps that is sustainable. If you are not in the top tier market yet, you can figure out how to get your art into the hands of more people by repurposing your art for sale in more places.

Whether you have a camera phone or a high-dollar DSLR camera collecting dust in your closet, you can snap a high-resolution image of your piece that can turn into other products. The most common way is to make limited or open edition art prints and sell them at a lower price point than the original, but that's just a start.

Note cards, art trading cards, tote bags, and posters are just a few things you could do on your site with the art. I saw one artist who took all her art, put it into a magazine style layout and then created 'zines for fans to buy. Someone who likes your art, and wants it all, but has no budget, might enjoy a 'zine of your work. You could also use a 'zine to focus on a niche you exist in, share works of others, and post up links to your shop for people to buy after they've read your it.

You could take your image and have it laid across all kinds of products that you find in Zazzle, Society6, and the like. As mentioned in the DTP section, there's less work involved, but also less profit, so you will need to put in the effort to market your shop to make sure you get enough volume to be sustainable.

When a nonartist friend asked me if this technique was considered selling out, after hanging my head in disbelief, I shared with him a simple idea that I think all artists should consider. As a fine artist, we may gain fans of all income levels. They love our work, but cannot afford an original, or even a limited-edition print. For those fans, there are the lower priced options. Some artists might cringe at the idea of their work on a phone cover, but I choose to look at it as the highest form of fandom. If someone loves your work so much they are willing to carry it with them everywhere; I can't think of a higher compliment of your work.

HIGH-LEVEL CREATION

Now, these ideas are great, and I hope they get your wheels turning, but what about some really high-level content and product creation ideas? The following ideas are more advanced, will take a lot of work and time to get started, but the end result could reap bigger rewards than doing one-to-one sales on any marketplace. Read through these ideas, let them percolate, and if they apply, dig in. If you don't like these exact ideas, maybe they will bring other ideas to light.

MEMBERSHIP PROGRAM
Create an online program where people buy into your wisdom and experience. Some people are more than willing to pay a premium fee for getting complete access to that same full-length video from before (no time-lapse), along with super-detailed instructions on your process. I gave this idea to a client who told me it was too much work for little return. I said, "Tell that to the Bob Ross* estate."

FROM ART TO BOOK

Pick out a dozen or more images of art you created. Write a short story that goes along with the art. Turn that story and art into a book and put it up for sale on sites like Magcloud, Lulu, or Blurb.com.

If your work is more illustrative in nature, consider making a children's book that's filled with illustrations, but instead of being colorized, use line drawings and turn it into a coloring book.

FROM BOOK BACK TO ART

Follow up the book idea and make art prints from one or two of the pieces in the book, or do an entire series of limited-edition prints from your book art. Combine that imagery on high-quality paper, mix with quotes from the book, and put those up for sale as art prints. Taking it a step further, you can upload art into Zazzle and set up a custom text area on the page where customers can add their own information, like a quote they like, or a person's name.

ART OF THE MONTH CLUB

You could offer your work as a monthly subscription at a moderate price point. Customers would get a set print each month depending on when they subscribed, keep some for themselves, or give them away as gifts. The best part about this idea is that you can start small, take sales early, and at the end of that first month, send out the first print based on how many sales you had up to that moment. The initial buyers created the seed money for the first round of prints, and hopefully, a little more to help marketing the project to the next round of subscribers.

HOST A WORKSHOP

Your fans know you have the skills to paint, draw, or design. Given the opportunity, they'd jump at the chance to learn from you directly. Host a workshop in your area where people come together to craft their own projects, learn from each other, and make new friends. These can be intimate events, or bigger parties depending on how much you feel you can accomplish, but the end result is finding a group of people willing to pay money to sit in the same room as you and learn from someone they admire.

Brie Emery of Design Love Fest is a genius at this. She hosts Photoshop for bloggers workshops all over the country, and her fans relish the chance to hang out with her for the afternoon.

THE TAKEAWAY

There is no such thing as "passive income", which so many people claim exists on the Internet. You have an abundance of choices and opportunities to make more revenue from your work, but it will be <u>work</u>. Some are easier, and more hands off than others, but you will put lots of time and energy into this. However, if you pay attention and look for new opportunities when they present themselves, you will find ways to build upon your resources, and give yourself ways to make income with a little less work than hustling one art piece at a time.

Ask yourself, are you an artist, or are you an art business? You can be both, but to be successful you need to think and act like a business owner. There's a reason "starving artist" is a cliché; it's more often true than not. Contrast that with how often you have heard anyone refer to themselves as a starving business owner—not likely. If a successful, flourishing art business is what you want, then now is the time to start treating the work like *work*.

* Bob Ross is an American artist known for teaching a wet on wet process on the popular PBS series, *Joy of Art*. He is also known for his soothing demeanor, and the most epic afro in the art world. Although he donated many of his paintings, he made millions from his training courses.

CHAPTER 9

FURTHER DOWN THE RABBIT HOLE

As promised, I want to talk to you about your sales funnel, but before I do, we need to talk about digital sharecropping. I wasn't sure where this section belonged in the book because it overlaps many of the topics already discussed. In some cases, it contradicts what I said, but I believe it is important to talk about further.

DIGITAL SHARECROPPING?

Traditional sharecropping is when a land owner leases portions of his land to others, allowing them to plant vegetation on a parcel in exchange for a portion of the harvest. The benefit to the land owner was a means to maximize his harvest by sharing the effort with others. The benefit to the sharecropper was that he got a harvest bounty at a fraction of the cost of buying land.

The biggest problem with sharecropping is that the sharecroppers did not own or control the land, and the land owner could change the rules of the arrangement at whim. Worse-case scenario, the land owner would sell the land, or kick the sharecropper off the land, and they would be left without any means to make a living, even if they had invested a lot of time and energy into the land.

Digital sharecropping is a new phrase that some are using to describe those of us who use other online systems to do our business. If you use Etsy, Zazzle, Facebook, Twitter, or any other online service that you do not own and operate, then you are a digital sharecropper. It's OK, we all do it a little, but there's a problem with this situation.

Let's say you start your day by logging into Facebook; you want to say hello to the thousands of fans you have accumulated over the years. You love Facebook for its connectivity and the ability to share your story, and you see no reason to be anywhere else. However, today you cannot login. Someone hacked your account and posted a bunch of SPAM and porn on your page, which caused major alarms all over, Facebook security locked you out, and shut down your page. In an instant, all that connectivity—all those fans are gone—you have zero social presence online.

This is an extreme case, and likely would not happen to you, but it could happen, and because you spent all your time harvesting crops on someone else's land, you were left with no way to connect to your hard-earned fan base.

I recall a story where a prominent seller on Etsy had the rug pulled out from under her in a similar manner. Granted, she was operating a business under auspicious means, creating derivative work based on copyrighted material, so it was only a matter of time before things caught up with her.

Someone had reported her shop to the Etsy authorities, and without warning, Etsy shut it down and gave her no recourse. On her blog, she complained that 90 percent of her income came from Etsy and that they had taken food out of her mouth (forget that it was stolen food). The blog post lit up with comments from supporters and detractors, gaining her a lot of notoriety, but no matter what side you sat, the issue remained that she went from being an Etsy big shot to nothing in a matter of minutes.

Had she spent less time on Etsy and more time building a loyal following on her e-mail list, selling more of her work on her own website, this would not have been as big an issue. It might have still hurt, but not killed her business completely.

Every single client I work with gets the same lecture from me about this subject. It is imperative that they focus their energy toward their own website, and implement an active e-mail list. To ignore this advice is gambling with your future. Etsy, Facebook, Society6, and Twitter are not going anywhere soon, but that doesn't mean you cannot be left in the cold if they decide to cut you loose.

Truly successful creative businesses have an ongoing relationship with their fans through their website and e-mail list. Until you start collecting names onto your list, those people you sell to on Etsy are not your customers; they are Etsy's customers who just happened to buy something from you. Even if you could gather e-mail addresses from Etsy's database, it is against their terms of service for you to contact them about anything unrelated to the product they bought. However, you can inspire the customer to join your list through other means, which we will discuss in a moment.

I am not saying you must stop selling on other sites to sell strictly on your website. In fact, I think you should keep your shops open on those other platforms, even after you become successful through your own website. Marketplaces and social media will still bring an opportunity to attract people to your work, and this gives you a chance to bring them to your site for all the awesomeness they are missing elsewhere.

THE GOLD IS IN THE LIST

There's a common business axiom that reads, "The money is in the list," which is accurate, but a bit smarmy because it equates the people on your e-mail list to dollar bills. Instead, I like to say that the gold is in the list because the value of every person on my list is golden on several levels. They are dedicated fans, they give me the feedback I need to improve, and they will buy from me when I put out new work because they support my efforts. They are as precious to me as gold, and I treat them as such.

Through my list, I give my knowledge away freely because if it helps them grow their business, which equates to a success for me as well. I foster community through my list by bringing people together, either through the creators I feature, or by connecting one fan to another. I spread love through my list because I believe it is my duty to share the work of others who encourage other creative entrepreneurs to take action, improve their work, and follow their artistic dreams. My list is where the magic happens, and it can be that way for you.

Your Facebook, Twitter, and Instagram accounts could disappear tomorrow, but your list is always *your* list. No one, not even your e-mail autoresponder service can take that list away from you. You started it, you fostered it, you cultivated it, and you watched it grow. If you want to move it somewhere, you download it and take it somewhere. All those fans in one tidy place to take along anywhere you go. You can't do that with Facebook or Etsy.

If you have not started an e-mail list yet, I encourage you to start today. Go to Mailchimp, sign up for a free account and get going. I already know your next statement, "I don't know what to write about."

To which I reply, "doesn't matter, do it anyway," because deciding what to share is less important than getting started. Once you get started, you can figure out what to write about. That is a hefty conversation that doesn't fit here, but one web search for "what to write for my e-mail list" will give you plenty of content to sift through. If you have adoring fans, they are going to love anything you send, even if it is just to say, "Hi, here's what's up with the shop…"

THE SALES FUNNEL

The elusive beast I've been teasing you with for several pages is finally here, and I can guarantee it's a lot less interesting than you expect, but suck it up and listen because this could transform your outlook on business.

When you think of how you move customers through your

business, imagine a marble rounding the walls of a funnel until it hits the undeniable port at the bottom. When new potential customers come sniffing around, they may not be inclined to jump right into your highest priced products. In fact, they may not even buy your lowest priced product at first, but if you can seduce them with your brand, your style, and your personality, you may have an opportunity to get them into a shopping cart soon enough.

Imagine a customer comes to your shop and they find their way to your blog. They see your updates about the latest pieces, maybe a process video, or a rant about spending too much time on work and not enough fun with family. They like what you say, and they want more. In the sidebar, you have a special offer—a free how-to guide for the mere exchange of an e-mail address. They sign up immediately, and the marble enters the rim of the funnel.

A week later, they get your first e-mail update. You slipped their mind for a second, but they are happy to get this update. On it is a picture of your latest masterpiece and they love it. The love it even more because it's an affordable limited-edition. They don't buy yet, but a couple weeks later you send an announcement that your limited-editions are selling fast. With a sense of urgency, they jump over to your shop, sees the print still in her cart and buys without blinking. You ship the piece, nicely wrapped, toss in a thank you note with a special coupon code for any piece over $50, and share with a friend for another coupon code.

Coincidentally, your customer has a birthday for a family member coming up and thinks one of your originals would be a good gift. It's a lot of money for them, but the coupon code helps. She buys, gets the new package in the mail. She loves the packaging, loves the special thank you note you sent, again, and loves the painting even more. She keeps the painting and instead buys a print for the family member. The thank you note mentions you are publishing a book of your work and you have a new Kickstarter campaign to get it finished.

Checking out the Kickstarter, she may not want a copy of the book, but she loves what you do, wants to support you, and she shares it with all her friends on Facebook. She also writes about you on her own site, which just happens to be a popular interior design blog. You post up a special notice for new influx of readers, letting them know you are grateful for them visiting from that blog post, and any friend of them is a friend of yours. You create a special limited-edition print for those people, and it sells out instantly.

Of all the new fans, a few start asking you how you do what you do, and would you be willing to share techniques. You get an idea for a course about your technique, create some videos and training materials with some help from friends. You put it up for sale on your site for $99, and share it with your fans. You send an e-mail to your list, and drop a note to your customer with the popular design blog. She tells her fans about the course, and as the marble drops through the port at the bottom, you enroll 50 people in the first month.

Welcome to your new life.

CHAPTER 10

YOUR TIME IS NOW

If you didn't know anything about how to sell your art online before this, or were confused where to start, now you have more reference material in your pocket. With each of the categories and sites I discussed, you get winners and losers, but there is no clear-cut choice for everyone. You must gauge the level of involvement you want to have with your product versus how much profit you want to keep. Simply put, it's time and effort versus money.

The sites mentioned in this book are just the tip of the iceberg. As the Internet grows, more and more sites will come to offer up different and better alternatives, and existing sites will evolve. You must question what works for you and your art. The only way to find out which sites you should use is to get out there and do it.

"REAL ARTISTS SHIP"

That's more than a popular quote by Steve Jobs, it's a lifestyle choice. As I mentioned in the beginning of the book, don't be a victim of analysis paralysis. Do not overthink your choices or plague yourself with inaction. It's better to act and get it wrong than to sit back, dwell, tweak, and get nothing. The more time you spend deciding what to do is less time you are sharing your art and making money. Pick one site right now and go post something. You will not get it right the first time, or maybe not the second, but in time you will see sales.

The moment of that first sale is, and like an addict you will chase that dragon to your next sale, and your next one. Embrace that feeling, own it like a right of passage, and never stop working toward your dream.

I thank you for reading this book, and I hope it has helped inspire and inform you. Actually, I want more from you than that. What would make this book worthwhile to me is to see that you took what you learned and applied it. If after reading this, you opened your first shop, or you looked into new ways to sell your work, I want to know about it. You can e-mail me direct: dave@freshrag.com. I cannot guarantee I will answer every e-mail, but I will try hard.

No more waiting around—go get to work! Your future success inspires me.

APPENDIX

RELATIVE LINKS

1XRUN
www.1xrun.com

20X200
www.20x200.com

ART FINDER
www.artfinder.com

ARTFIRE
www.artfire.com

ARTIST RISING
www.artistrising.com

BEHANCE
www.behance.net

BIG CARTEL
www.bigcartel.com

CAFE PRESS
www.cafepress.com

CARGOH
www.cargoh.com

COGO HOUSE
www.cogohouse.com

DEVIANT ART
www.deviantart.com

EBAY
www.ebay.com

ENVATO
www.envator.com

ETSY
www.etsy.com

FAB
www.fab.com

FINE ART AMERICA
www.fineartamerica.com

GIGPOSTERS
www.gigposters.com

GRAPHIC RIVER
www.graphicriver.net

GUMROAD
www.gumroad.com

IMAGEKIND
www.imagekind.com

INKD
www.inkd.com

ISTOCKPHOTO
www.istockphoto.com

MAILCHIMP
www.mailchimp.com

MAMMOTH & CO
www.mammoth.co

MEYLAH
www.meylah.com

PAPIRMASSE
www.papirmasse.com

PHOTO DUNE
www.photodune.net

RED BUBBLE
www.redbubble.com

SAATCHI
www.saatchiart.com

SERGEANT PAPER
www.sergeantpaper.com

SHOPIFY
www.shopify.com

SHUTTERSTOCK
www.shutterstock.com

SOCIETY6
www.society6.com

SPREADSHIRT
www.spreadshirt.com

STORENVY
www.storenvy.com

UNCOVET
www.uncovet.com

WORDPRESS
www.wordpress.org

ZAZZLE
www.zazzle.com

THAT WAS FUN, RIGHT?

NOW, CAN I ASK A FAVOR?

I hope you enjoyed this book, and you got some tremendous value from it. As an independent author, it's far more important to me than anything else that my readers get served. In order to serve you, I need to know what you like.

It is also important to me that this book gets into the hands of more artists who need it. Many of those who have read this book said it changed the way they looked at their art, treating it like a business. The way I get this book into more hands is with reviews. Reviews are the basis for this book's livelihood on the different places it's sold, so this is where I ask you to use the link below to quickly give your rating and thoughts about *Selling Art Online*. It will only take a few seconds, and you be doing me a solid. Thanks!

www.freshrag.com/rate-sao/

THE LESSONS DON'T STOP

MORE INSIGHT DIRECT TO YOU

If you're this far along, then I assume you *really* enjoyed the book, and that makes me happy, but maybe it makes you a little sad because this lesson is done ... or is it? What if I told you that you could continue to get lessons like these served weekly for free?

Join the Fresh Rag Newsletter and each week(ish) I will deliver you stories, techniques, lessons learned from others about how to make headway in the ever-changing world of selling art in the online environment.

Want to know what changes are up at Etsy or Facebook? We'll talk about it. Curious to find out the next hot new social media tool, or a new approach to making your work stand out from the crowd? We'll go there. Maybe you just want to know what book, show, or adventure I have coming out next. Don't worry, there is plenty of that for you.

Come join the fun, interact, and share your own tale. Who knows, your story may end up inspiring others in a future update.

www.freshrag.com/news/

LEARN FROM THE PROS

CREATIVE STIMULATION VIA HEADPHONES

In June of 2013, I embarked on a journey to get my message out to the creative people of the world. I started a weekly show called The Creative Business Podcast—The NO BS, Straight Talk Approach to Earning More From Your Creative Pursuits. The show started strong and has gotten better with each guest we feature.

In April of the next year, I reinvented the show to be even better, and changed the name. I brought in guests who already found success in their own businesses, lending insight, sharing stories, and providing a path for the rest of us to follow.

The Fresh Rag Show was born from the concept that no artist shall ever feel desperate or alone, that we all fight the same battles, and the obstacles we encounter can be conquered. I made this show for you—come join the fight.

www.freshrag.com/podcast/

ABOUT THE AUTHOR

Dave Conrey is an artist, designer, entrepreneur, and family man. When not spending time with his son, playing dinosaurs or superheroes, he is working on a number of creative projects, ranting on his podcast (The Fresh Rag Show), or writing his next book. Before launching his own brand, he worked for two decades as a graphic designer and art director, and he uses this experience to inform, engage, and advise creative entrepreneurs on how to take their work from a hobby to a viable business. To find out more, **visit www.freshrag.com** to see what he has planned next.

SELLING ART ONLINE

21102963R00047

Made in the USA
San Bernardino, CA
05 May 2015